First Words and Numbers

Miles Kelly

First published in 2016 by Miles Kelly Publishing Ltd
Harding's Barn, Bardfield End Green, Thaxted, Essex, CM6 3PX, UK

2 4 6 8 10 9 7 5 3

Publishing Director Belinda Gallagher
Creative Director Jo Cowan
Editorial Director Rosie Neave
Senior Editor Sarah Parkin
Senior Designer Rob Hale
Cover Designer Joe Jones
Production Elizabeth Collins, Caroline Kelly
Reprographics Stephan Davis, Jennifer Cozens, Thom Allaway
Consultant Susan Purcell

ISBN 978-1-78617-018-7

Printed in China

British Library Cataloguing-in-Publication Data
A catalogue record for this book is available from the British Library

ACKNOWLEDGEMENTS
The publishers would like to thank the following artists who have contributed to this book:
Letters: Richard Watson, Numbers: Michael Garton, Words: Heather Heyworth, Animals: Nik Afia

Made with paper from a sustainable forest

www.mileskelly.net

Letters

Aa

apple

ant

astronaut

ambulance

anchor

a b c d e f g h i j k l m n

Bb

What colour is the balloon?

balloon

boy

bicycle

bus

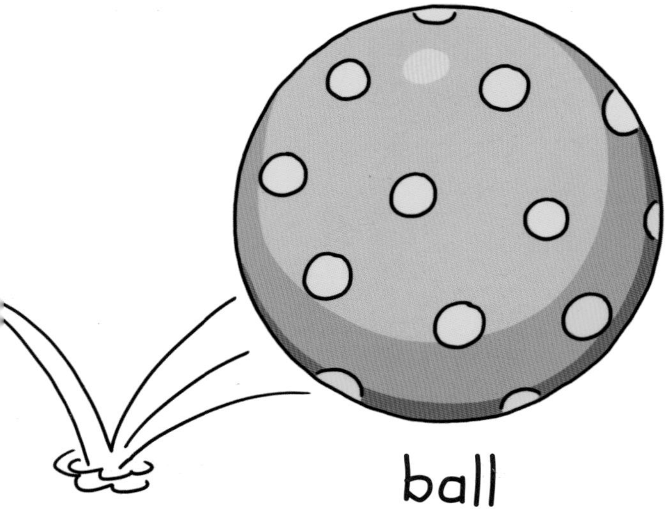

ball

book

butterfly

o p q r s t u v w x y z

Cc

car

clock

castle

How many candles are on the cake?

caterpillar

cow

cake

cat

a b c d e f g h i j k l m n

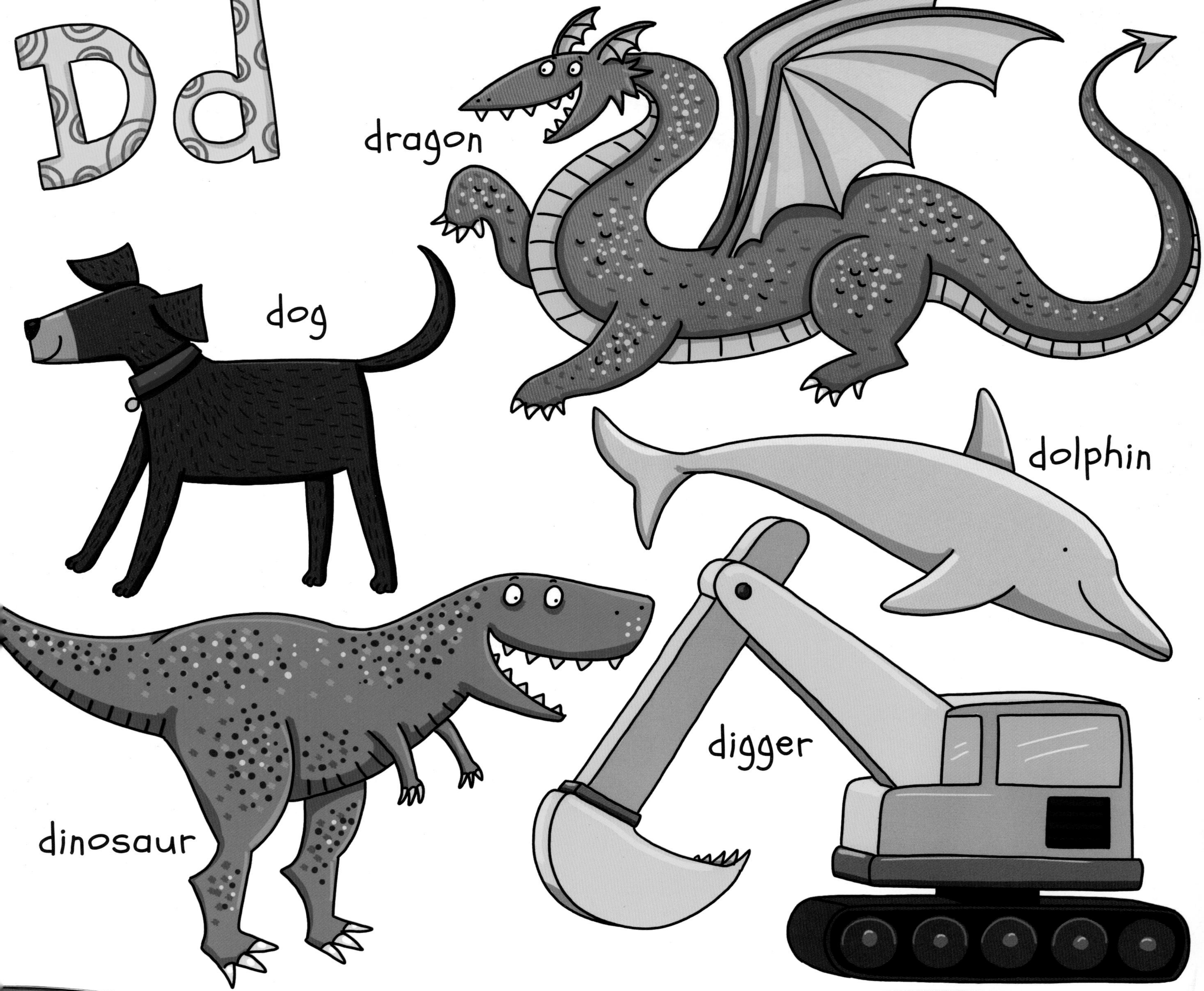
Dd
dragon
dog
dolphin
digger
dinosaur
o p q r s t u v w x y z

Ee

How many ears does the elephant have?

elephant

egg

elf

envelope

a b c d e f g h i j k l m n

Ff

fire

feather

fox

flower

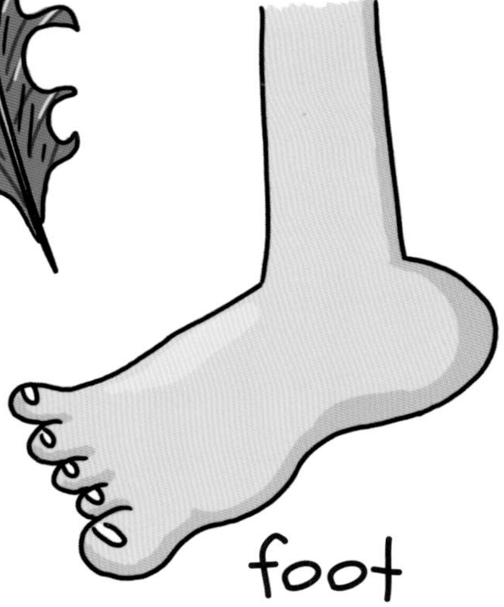

foot

fairy

fish

o p q r s t u v w x y z

Gg
goose
grapes
goat
What colour are the gloves?
girl
gloves
ghost
a b c d e f g h i j k l m n

Hh

helicopter

hen

hand

horse

hat

hair

head

o p q r s t u v w x y z

Ii
igloo
iguana
PARTY!
To
invitation
Jj
jigsaw
juice
jug
jewels
a b c d e f g h i j k l m n

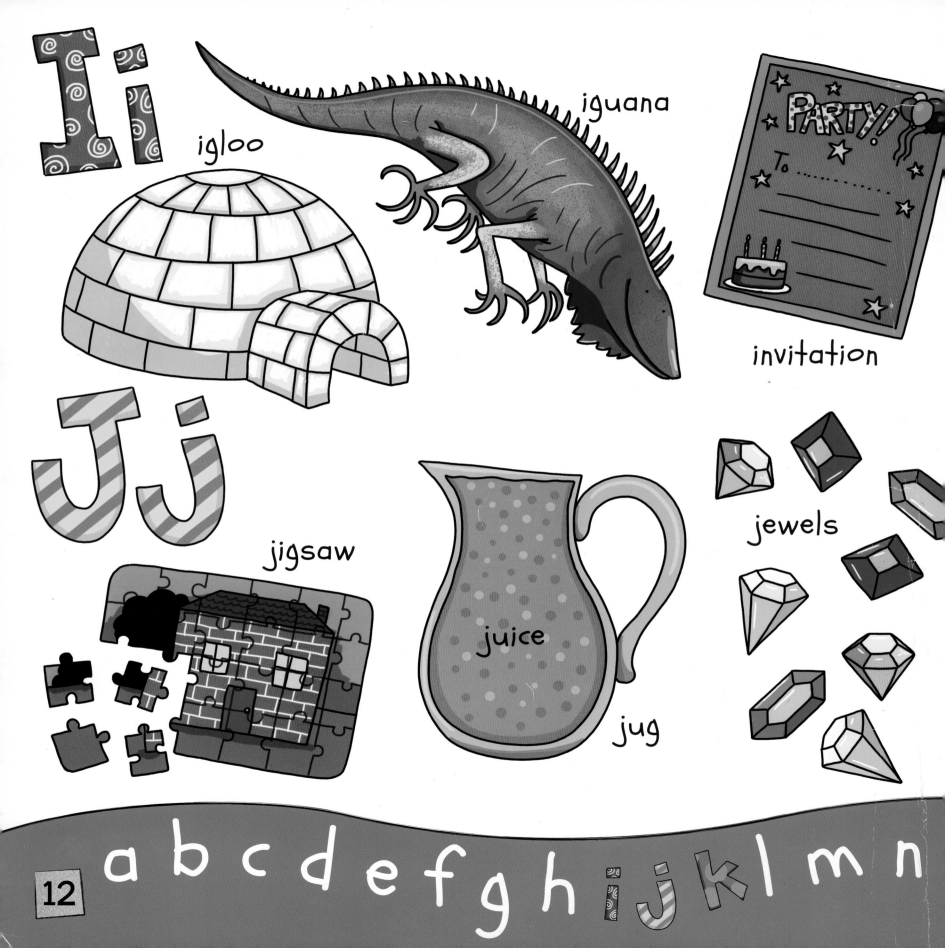

Kk

How many bows are on the kite?

o p q r s t u v w x y z

Ll

ladybird

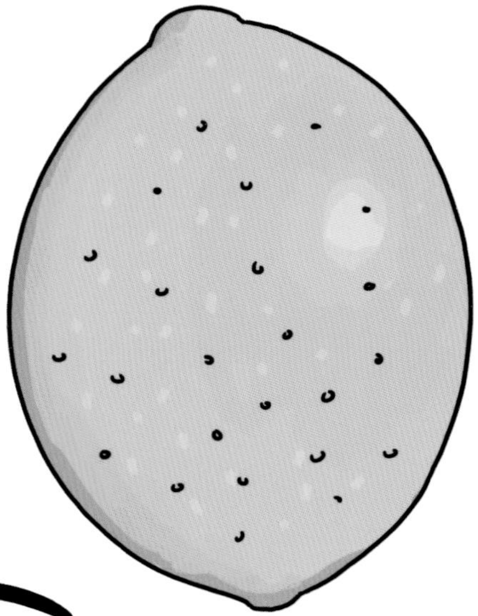

lemon

leaf

How many spots are on the ladybird?

lion

lamb

a b c d e f g h i j k l m n

Mm

mouse

moon

motorbike

Nn

nut

nurse

nest

o p q r s t u v w x y z

Oo

orange

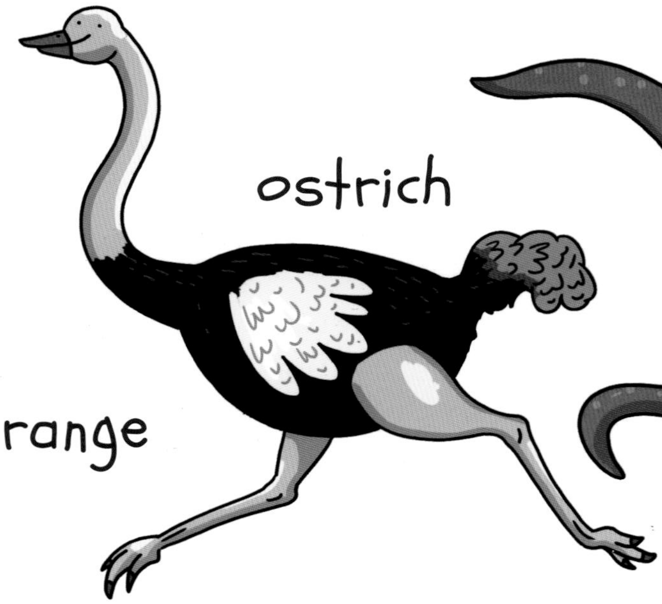

ostrich

octopus

Pp

pizza

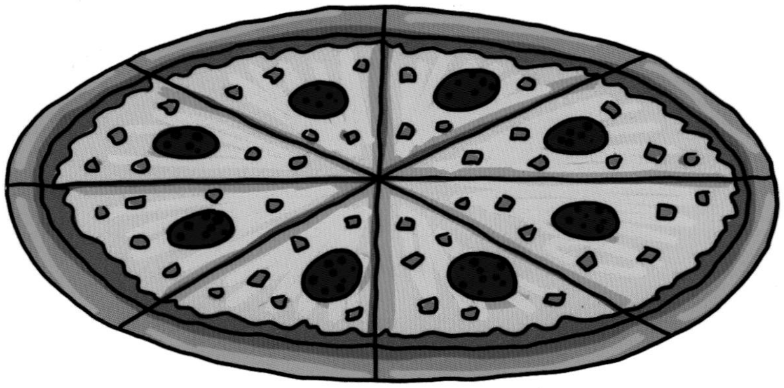

princess

present

a b c d e f g h i j k l m n

pirate
penguin
puppy
pencil
What colour is the princess's dress?
paper
paint
paintbrush
o p q r s t u v w x y z

Qq

quilt

question mark

queen

Rr

rabbit

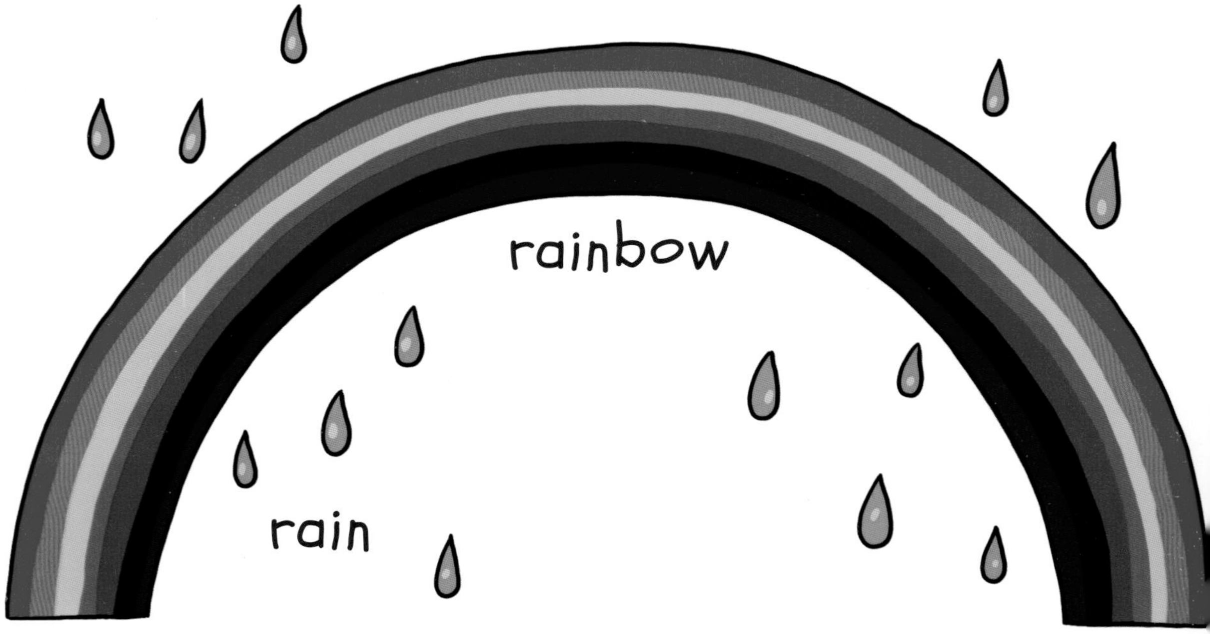

a b c d e f g h i j k l m n

ring

How many colours are in the rainbow?

robot

rocket

raspberry

rat

o p q r s t u v w x y z

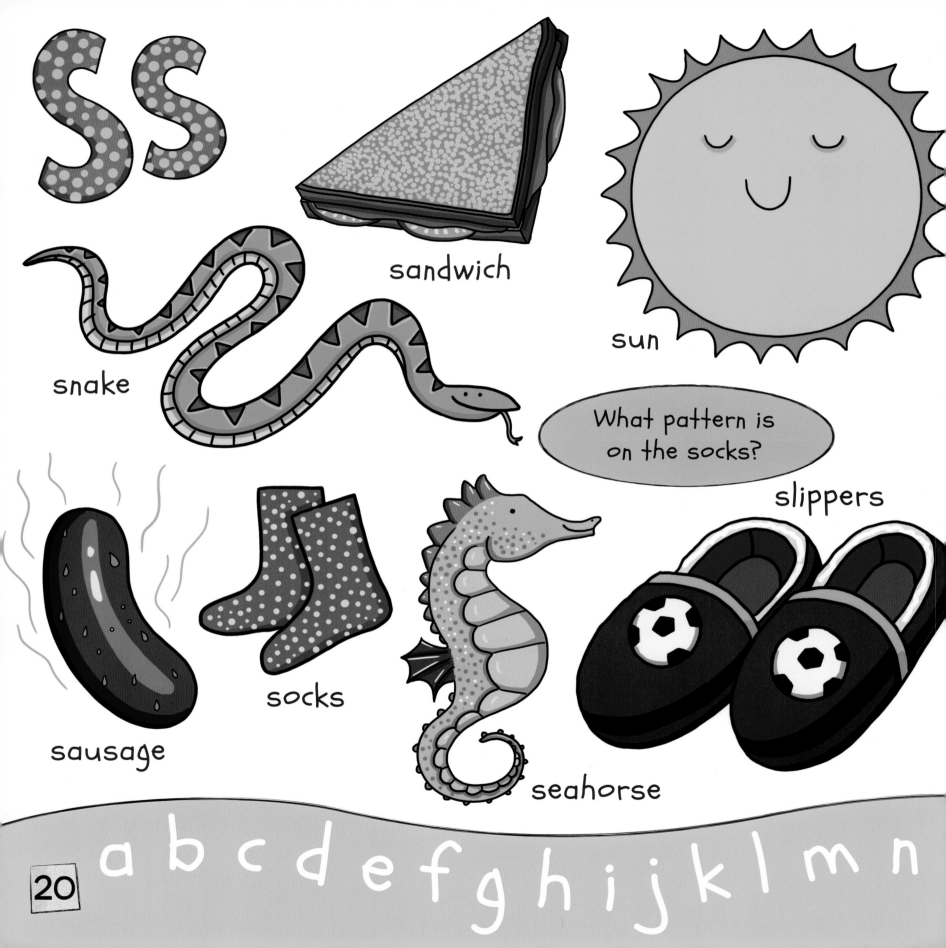

Ss

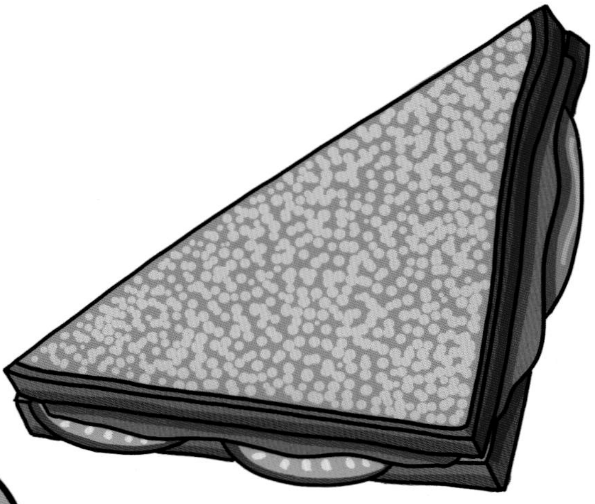

sandwich

sun

snake

What pattern is on the socks?

sausage

socks

seahorse

slippers

a b c d e f g h i j k l m n

Tt
train
tomato
teddy
tractor
tree
tiger
toothpaste
toothbrush
o p q r s t u v w x y z

Uu

up

upstairs

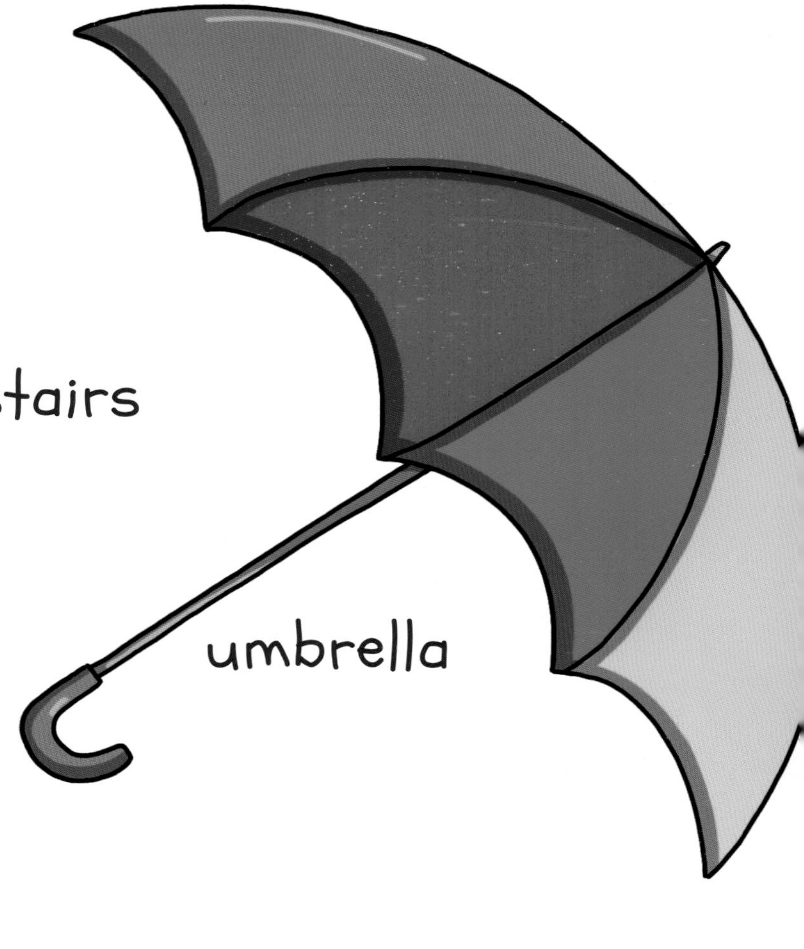

umbrella

Vv

vase

volcano

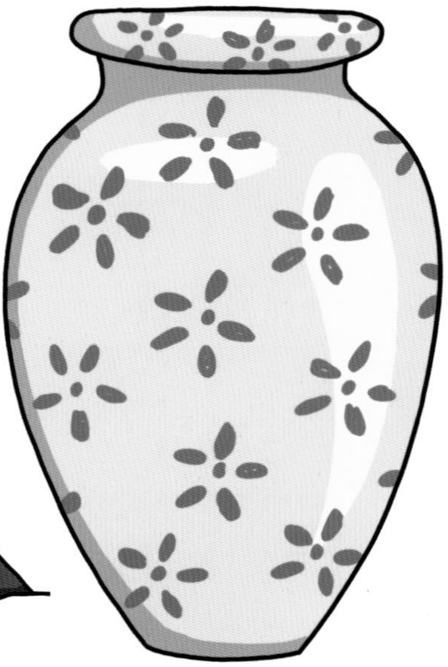

van

a b c d e f g h i j k l m n

Ww

watch

wheel

web

wand

What colour is the wizard's beard?

wizard

whistle

whale

o p q r s t u v w x y z

Xx

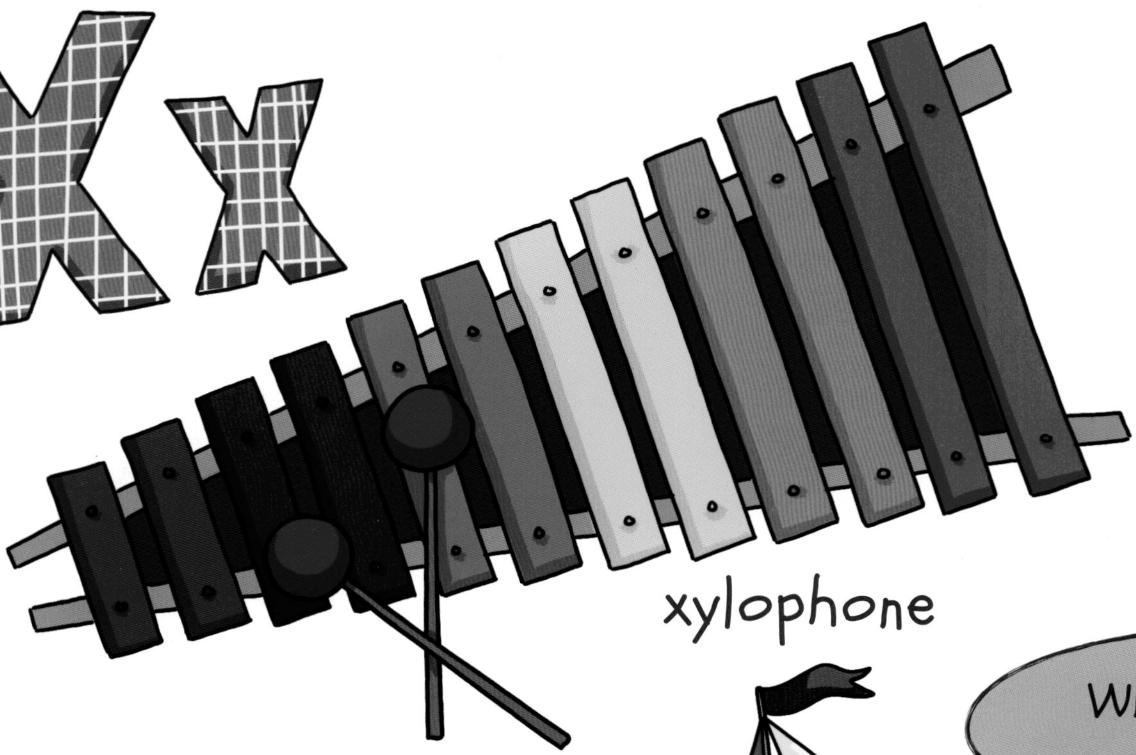

xylophone

x-ray

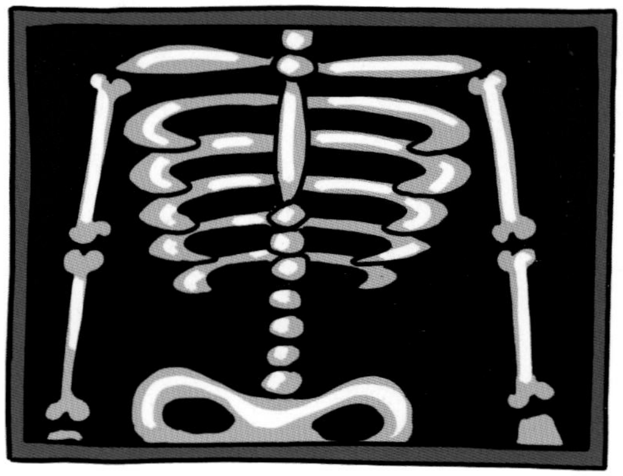

What colour is the yo-yo?

Yy

yoghurt

yacht

yo-yo

a b c d e f g h i j k l m n

Zz
zip
zigzag
zebra
zero
o p q r s t u v w x y z

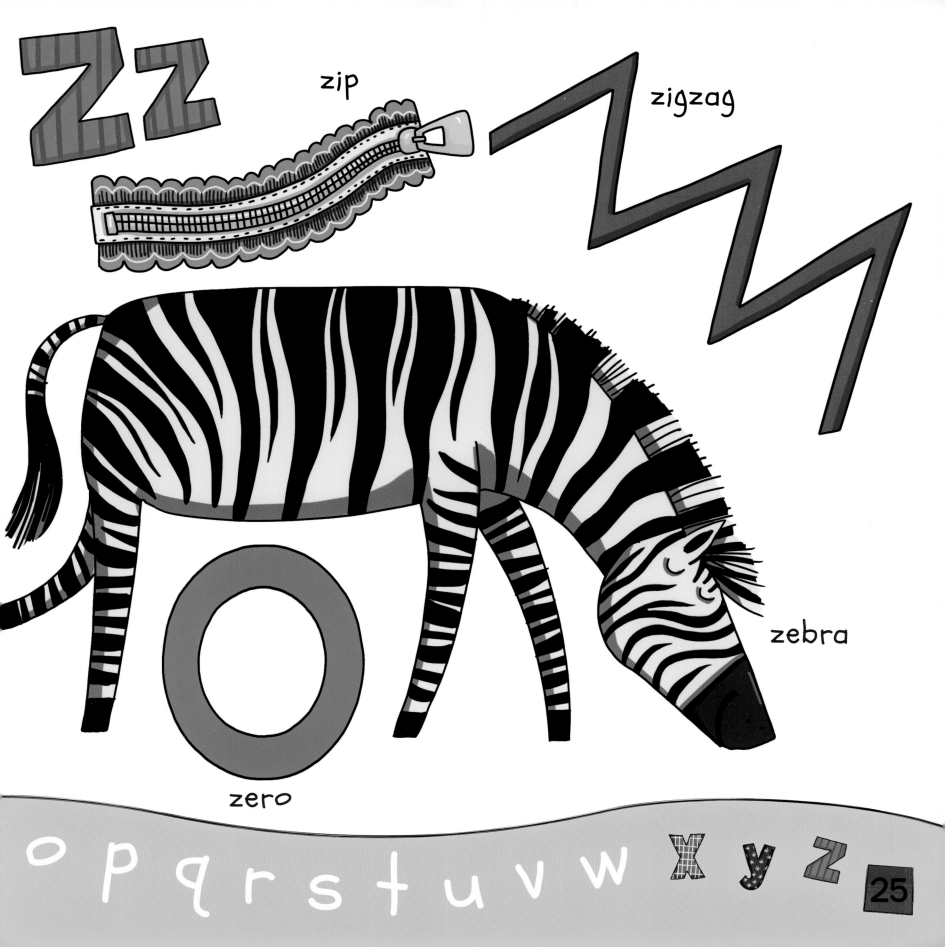

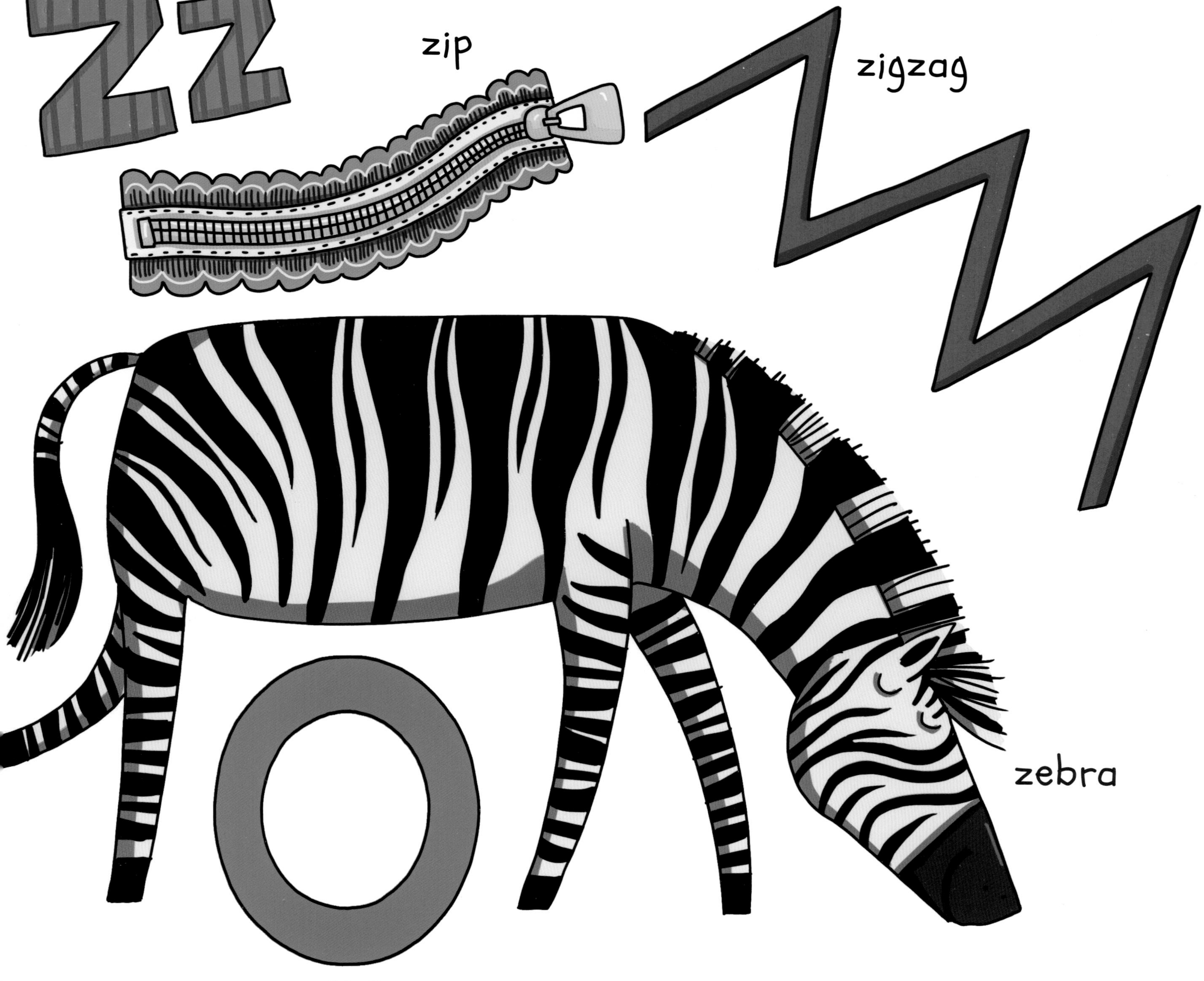

Can you find?

Look back on pages 4–25 to see if you can find the following things.

butterfly

fox

grapes

leaf

motorbike

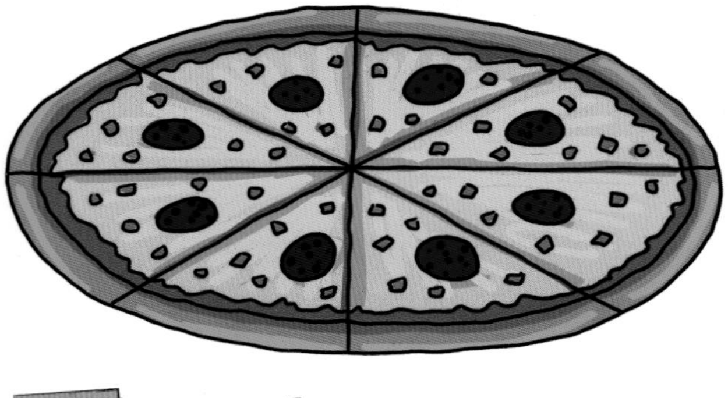

pizza

sun

umbrella

Numbers

1 comfy bed

one

What colour is the pillow?

Can you find?

1 lamp

1 clock

2 teddy bears

two

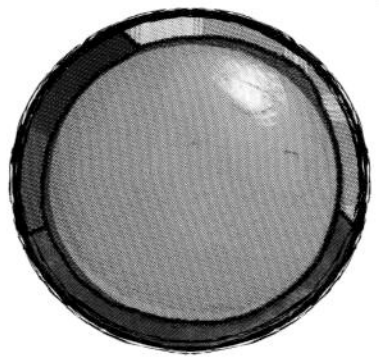

1 ball

2 books

2 pictures

3 racing go-karts

three

Can you find?

3 balloons

1 helter-skelter

4 carousel horses

four

What colour is the tasty candy floss?

 3 basketballs

 4 tents

 4 flags

5 party hats

five

I'm going to eat a cupcake!

Can you find?

5 candles

5 drinks

6 big balloons

six

How many blue balloons can you find?

6 cupcakes

4 presents

6 hot dogs

7 rubber rings

seven

How many pink swimming hats can you see?

Can you find?

1 lifeguard

7 floats

8 happy swimmers

eight

4 flip flops

5 towels

8 armbands

9 exercise books

nine

What shape is the clock on the wall?

WOOF!
Everyone needs a paintbrush!

Can you find?

1 teacher

10 paintbrushe

10 excited children

ten

9 pencils

6 lunchboxes

4 posters

11 woolly sheep

eleven

What is the cat chasing?

 Can you find?

 2 cats

 1 tractor

12 clucking chickens

twelve

 **4** mice

 **5** haystacks

 **3** cows

13 splashing fish

thirteen

Can you spot the caterpillar eating the leaf?
Remember, some of us might be hiding!

Can you find? 1 dragonfly 2 frogs

14 fluttery butterflies

fourteen

5 lily pads

6 flowers

4 bees

15 fifteen yellow bananas

Can you find?

9 apples

5 peppers

16 crunchy carrots

sixteen

What colour are the juicy apples?

2 trolleys

8 cherries

3 pineapples

17 tweeting birds

seventeen

Can you find?  2 kites  6 wheels

18 pretty flowers

eighteen

How many white flowers can you see?

4 clouds

3 trees

1 dog

19 waving flags

nineteen

How many red flags can you find?

Can you find?

1 ice cream

2 children

20 pink seashells

twenty

3 starfish

4 gulls

5 crabs

Can you find?

Look back on pages 28–47 to see if you can find the following things.

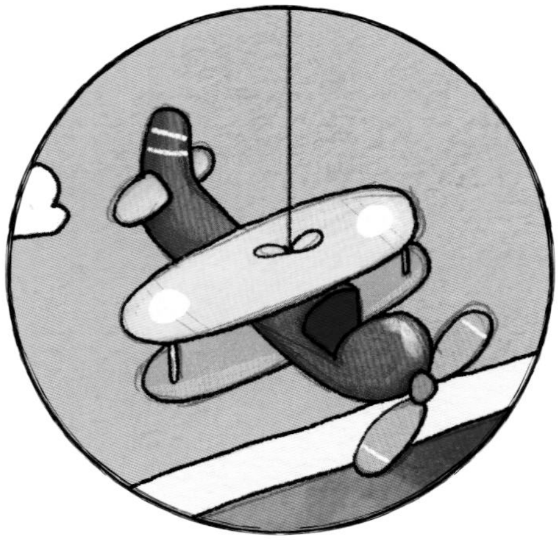

plane

cake

ball

clock

horse

basket

swings

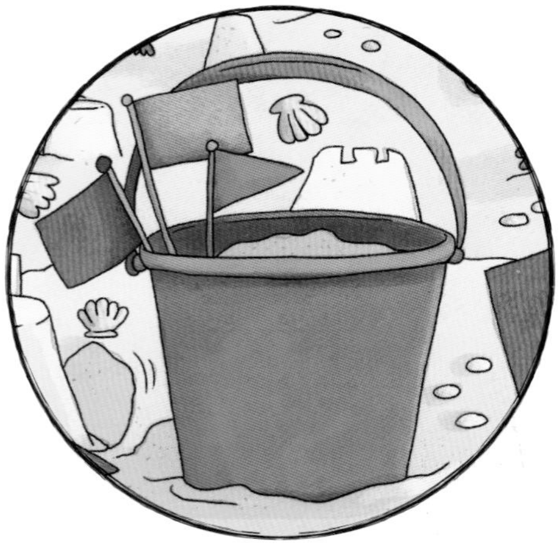

bucket

Words

At home

What colour are the curtains in the bedroom?

bathroom
toilet
sink
bath
television
window
door
sofa
lounge
How many of these objects have you got in your home?

In the home

Can you name the animal on the lamp?

Toys

car

jigsaw

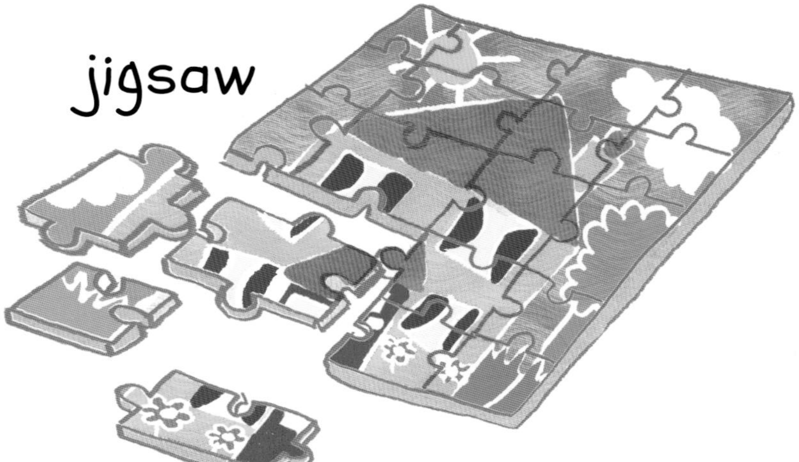

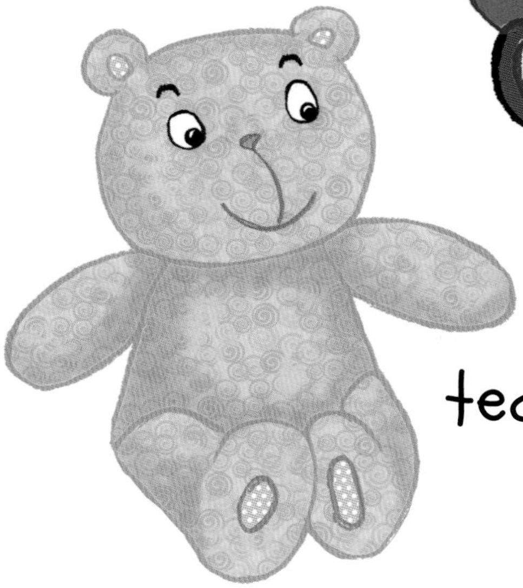

teddy

train

doll

dinosaur

blocks

What are your favourite toys to play with?

In the garden

How many carrots are growing in the garden?

What other things might be in a garden?

In the family

How many people are there in this family?

My body

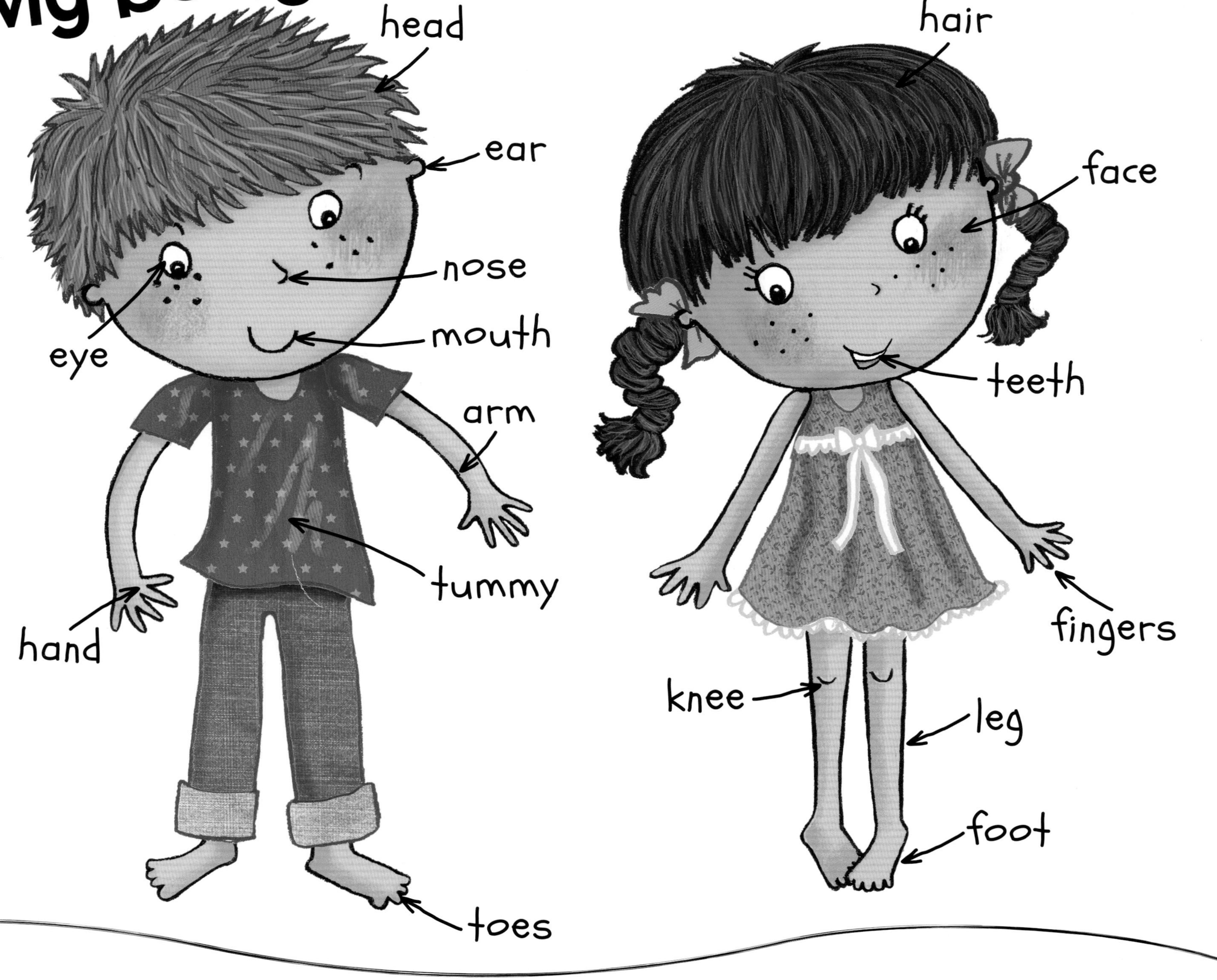

Can you point to these parts of your body?

On the street

What colour is the car?

Which shops do you like best?

Things that go

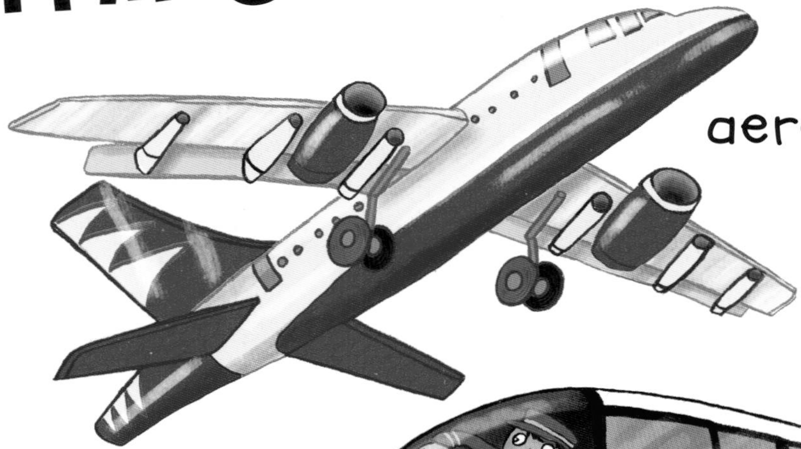

aeroplane

hot-air balloon

train

truck

tractor

How many of these vehicles can fly?

ambulance

helicopter

digger

ferry

fire engine

yacht

Which of these vehicles have you seen?

At the park

How many ducks can you see?

What do you like to do at the park?

Picnic food

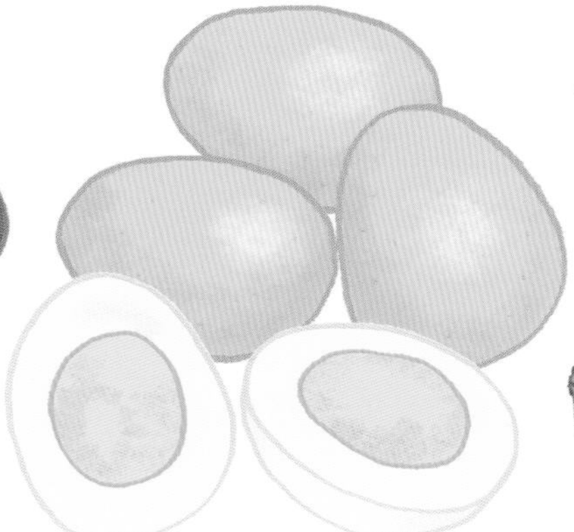

How many different foods are in the salad?

oranges
bananas
grapes
sweets
apples
cheese
strawberries
lettuce
salad
carrot
milk
pepper
cucumber
tomato
What food do you like to eat on a picnic?

On the beach

How many shells can you find?

What do you like doing on the beach?

Clothes

Which of these clothes do you wear when it is cold?

Colours

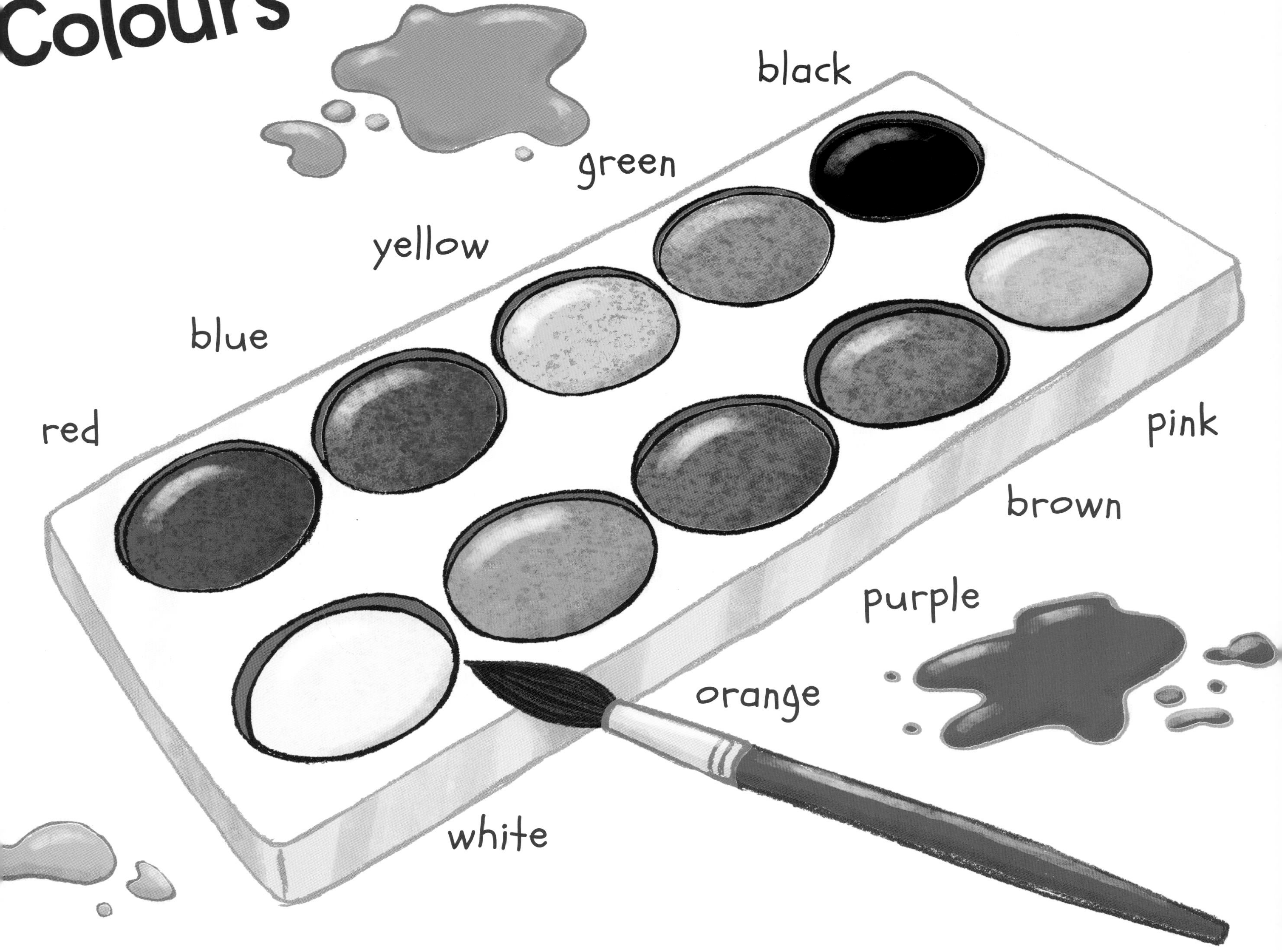

What colour clothes are you wearing?

Shapes

triangle

square

circle

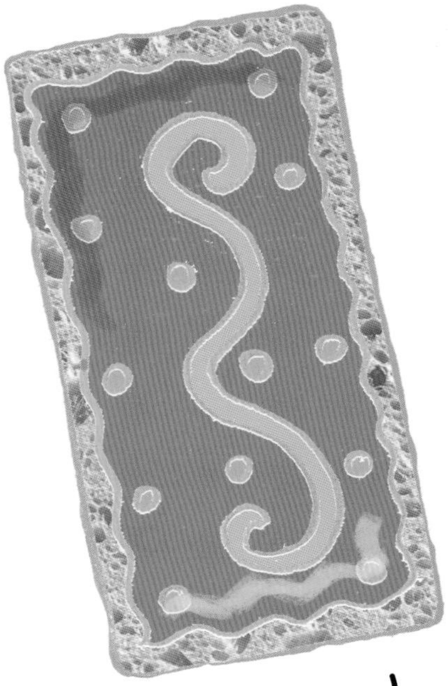

rectangle

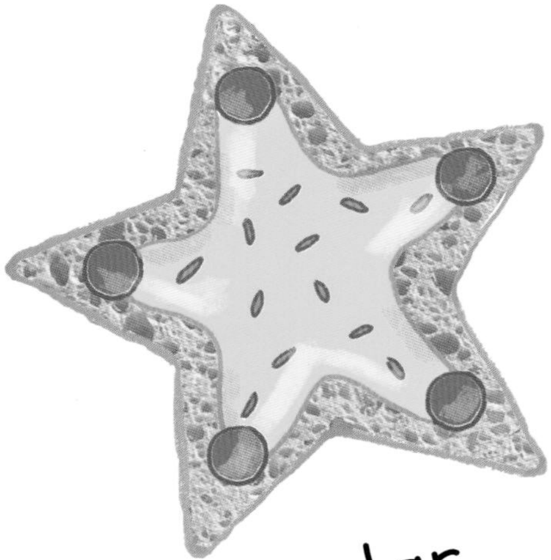

star

oval

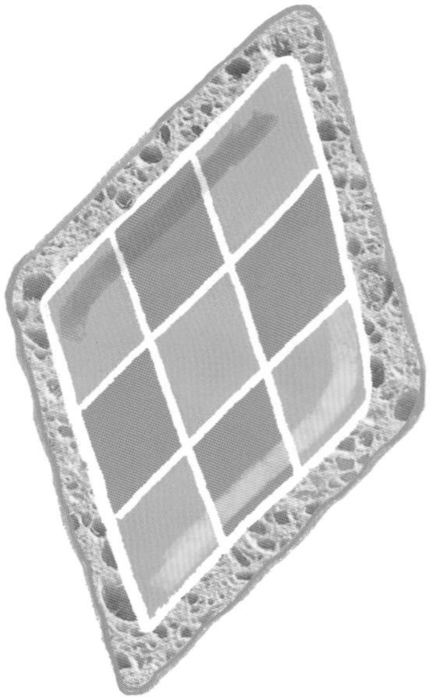

diamond

heart

What shape is an egg?

Numbers

Can you count all the way from one to twenty?

Can you find?

Look back on pages 50–71 to see if you can find the following things.

clock

teddy

dinosaur

hot-air balloon

yacht

sandwiches

sweets

t-shirt

Animals

Forests and woods

Eagles have sharp beaks and claws.

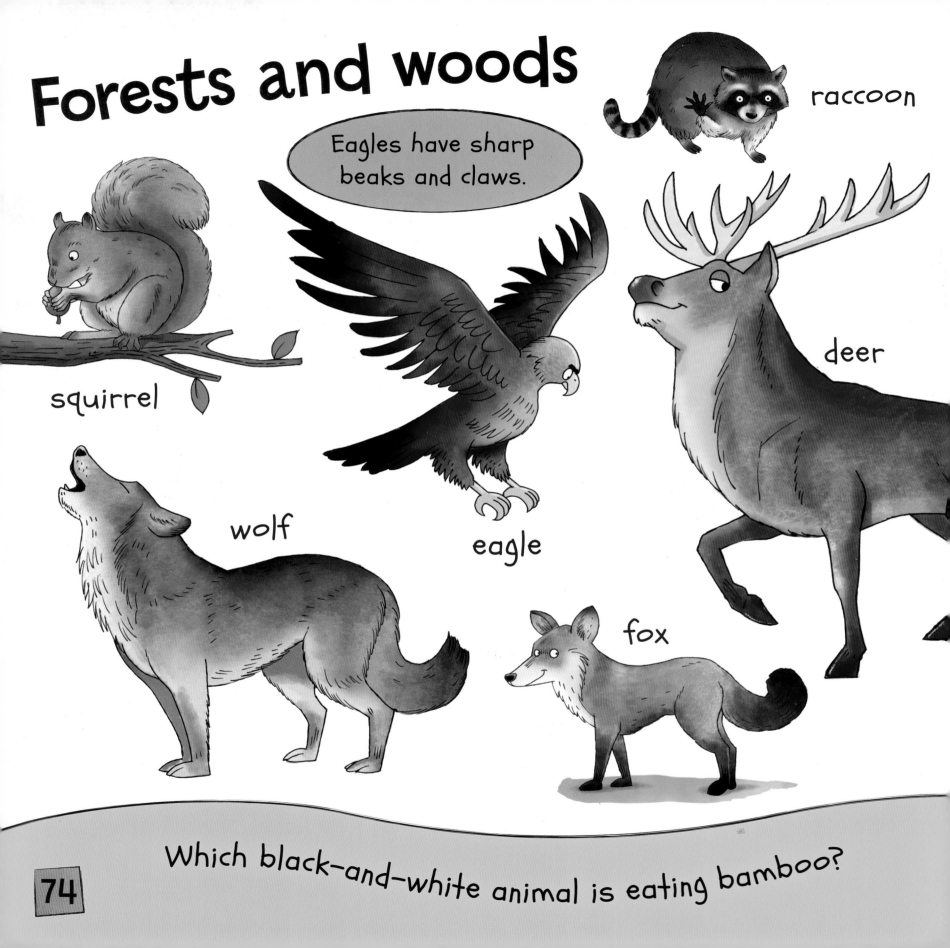

Which black-and-white animal is eating bamboo?

Giant pandas eat bamboo, which is a type of tall grass.

Which of these animals can fly?

Rivers and lakes

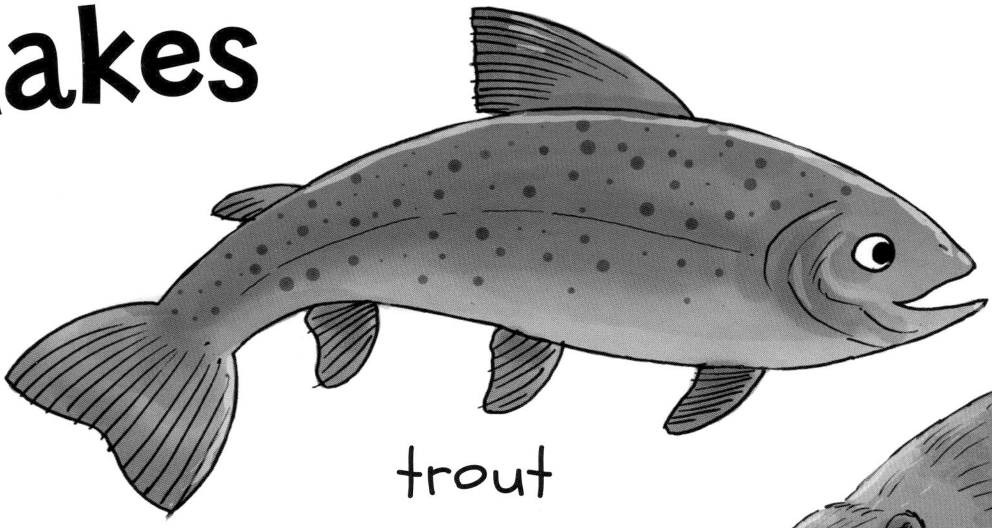

toad

trout

beaver

heron

kingfisher

Alligators hide in swampy water.

Which animal has pink feathers?

flamingo
pelican
Frogs have smooth, damp skin.
otter
alligator
swan
frog
How many of these animals are birds?

In the jungle

All snakes are meat eaters.

What kind of animal is a tarantula?

sloth
tree frog
monkey
macaw
tarantula
jaguar
chimpanzee
Tigers are the biggest cats.
tiger
tapir
chameleon
How many of these animals are cats?

On the seashore

gull

scallop

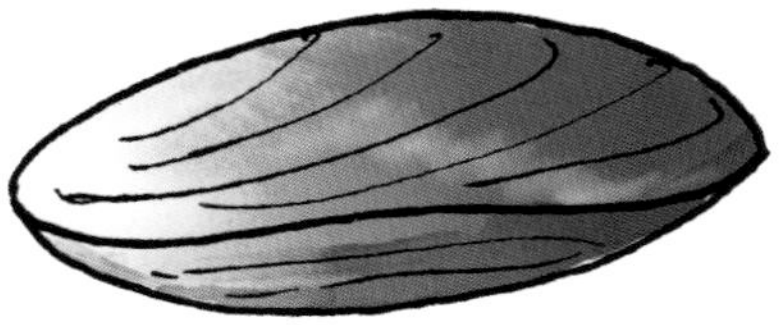

mussel

Sea anemones catch food with their tentacles.

sea anemone

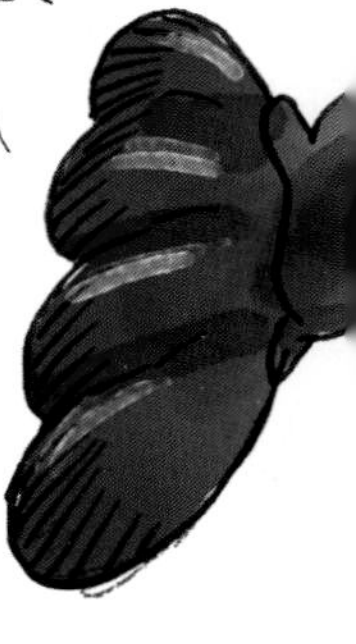

crab

starfish

Which animal has a body shaped like a star?

oystercatcher

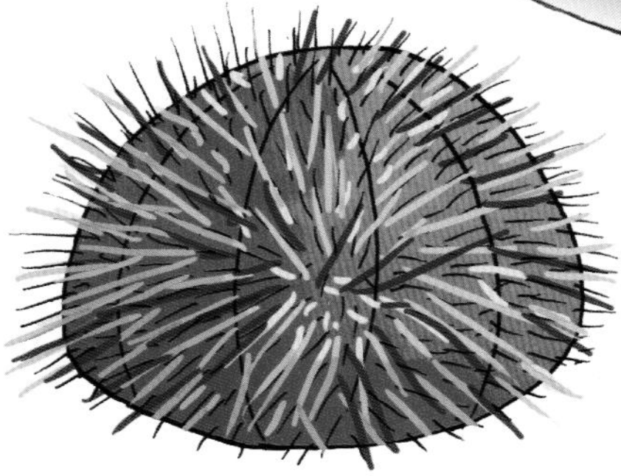

sea urchin

goby

Puffins can carry fish in their beaks.

puffin

lobster

How many of these animals have beaks?

Seas and oceans

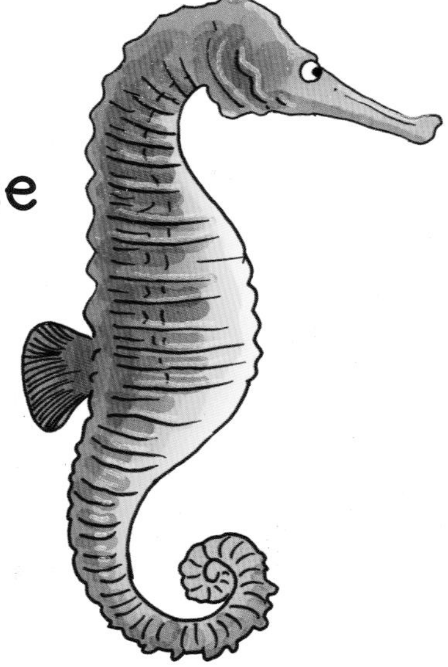

seahorse

blue whale

clownfish

turtle

The blue whale is the biggest animal in the world.

lionfish

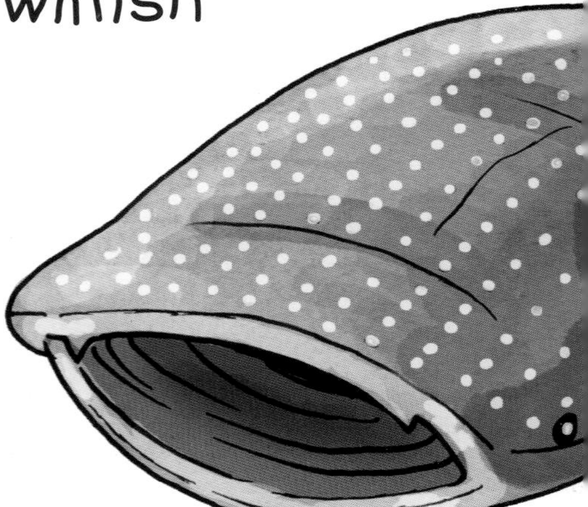

whale shark

Which fish looks like a spiky ball?

Pufferfish swallow water to make them swell up.

Which of these animals are sharks?

In the desert

fennec fox

camel

scorpion

Scorpions can survive without water for months.

lizard

kangaroo rat

sidewinder snake

Which animal has two large humps on its back?

Australian animals

Kangaroos jump using their back legs.

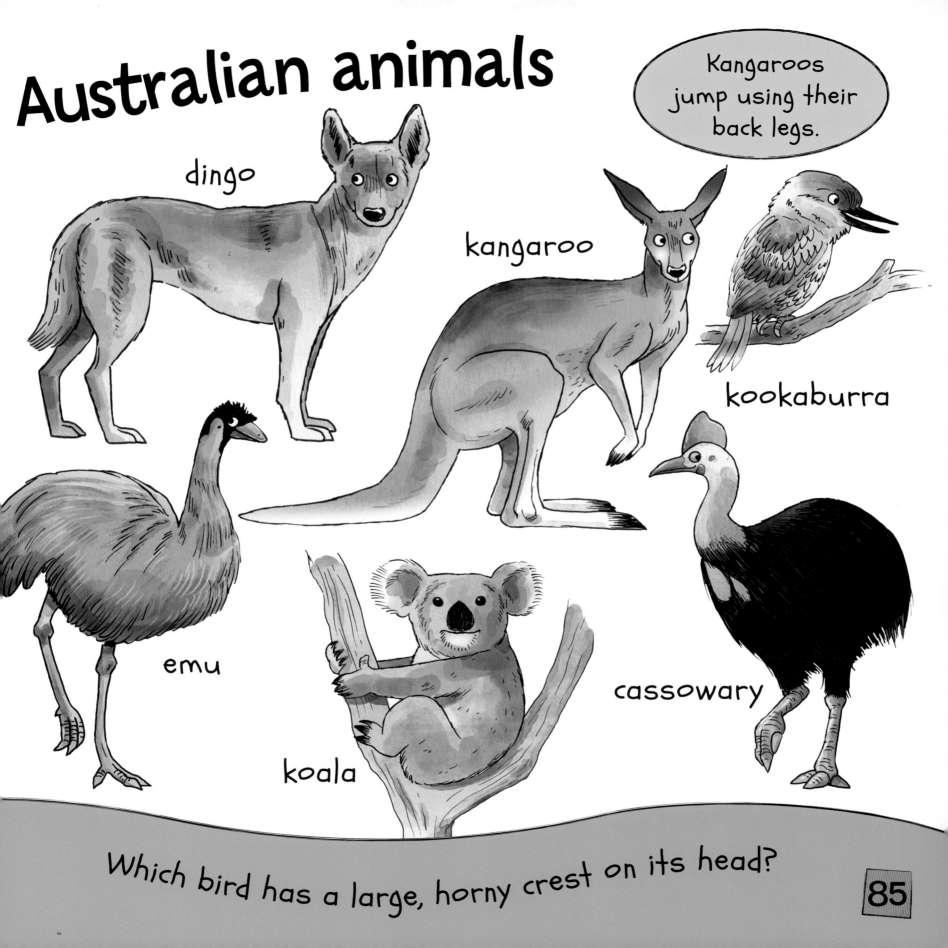

Which bird has a large, horny crest on its head?

African animals

Elephants are the biggest land animals.

Which animal has a long trunk?

cheetah
gazelle
baboon
Hippos wallow in rivers and swamps.
meerkat
hippopotamus
ostrich
zebra
giraffe
What is the tallest animal in the world?

In the Arctic

Polar bears are the biggest type of bear.

Which animal has two large tusks?

In the Antarctic

Which penguin is the biggest swimming bird?

On the farm

sheep

pig

goose

Sheep grow thick coats to keep them warm in winter.

cow

chicken

What is the name for a group of cows?

turkey

duck

goat

Ducks use their beaks to clean their feathers.

horse

Highland bull

donkey

How many of these animals have you seen?

Minibeasts

moth

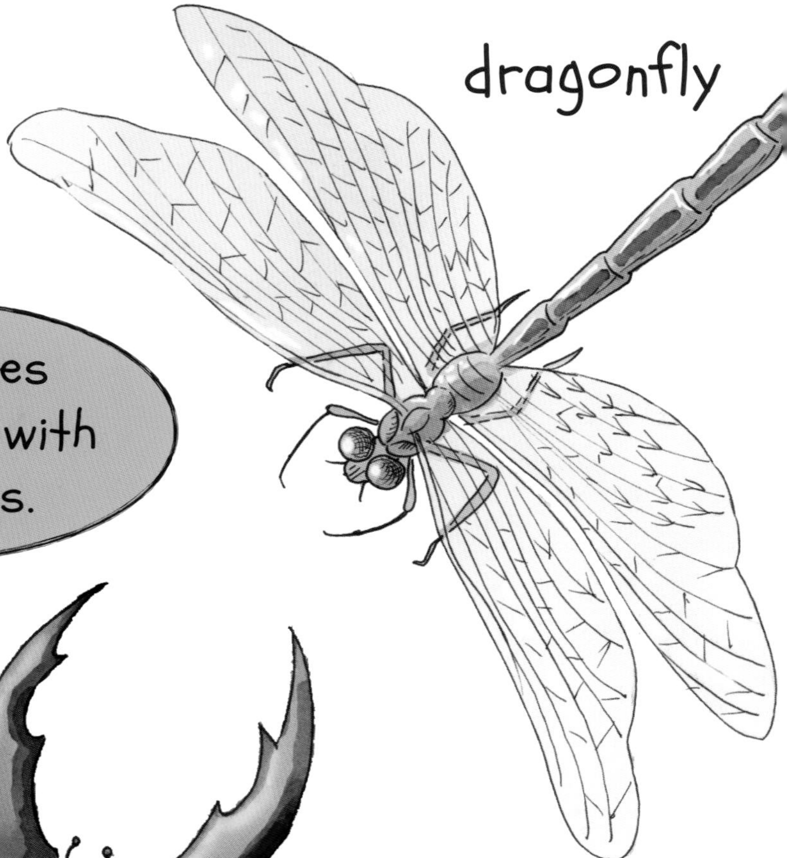

dragonfly

Dragonflies catch food with their legs.

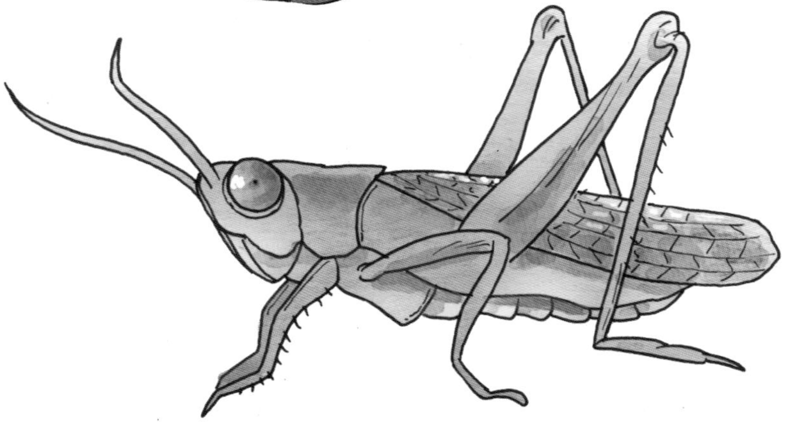

grasshopper

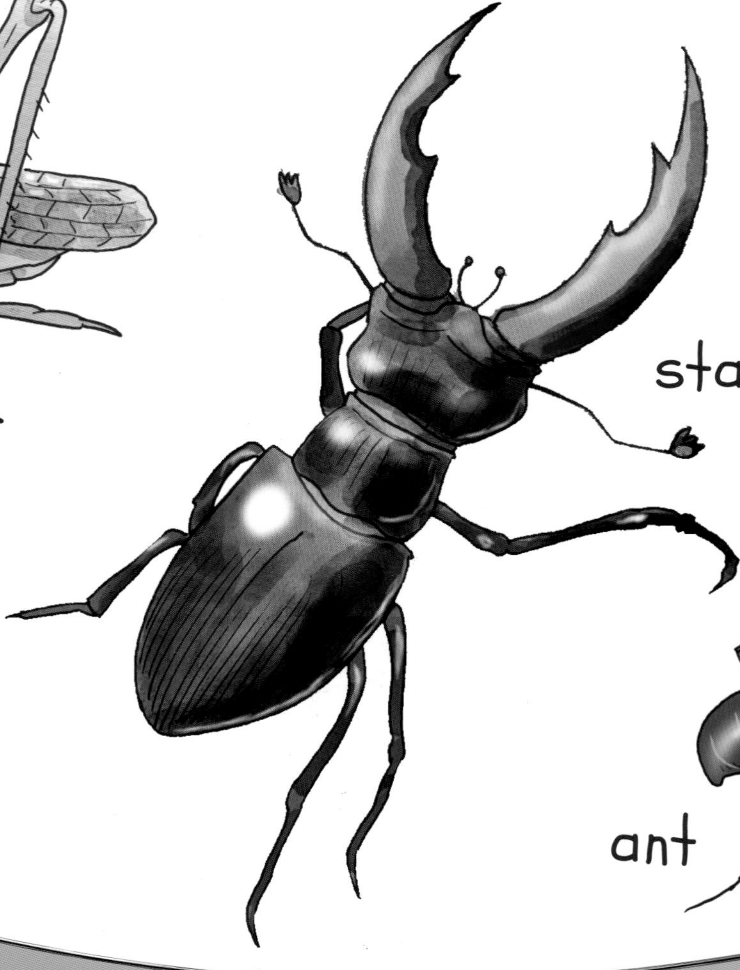

stag beetle

bee

ant

Which minibeast is red with black spots?

caterpillar
centipede
spider
snail
ladybird
fly
Butterflies are often brightly coloured.
praying mantis
butterfly
What does a caterpillar turn into?

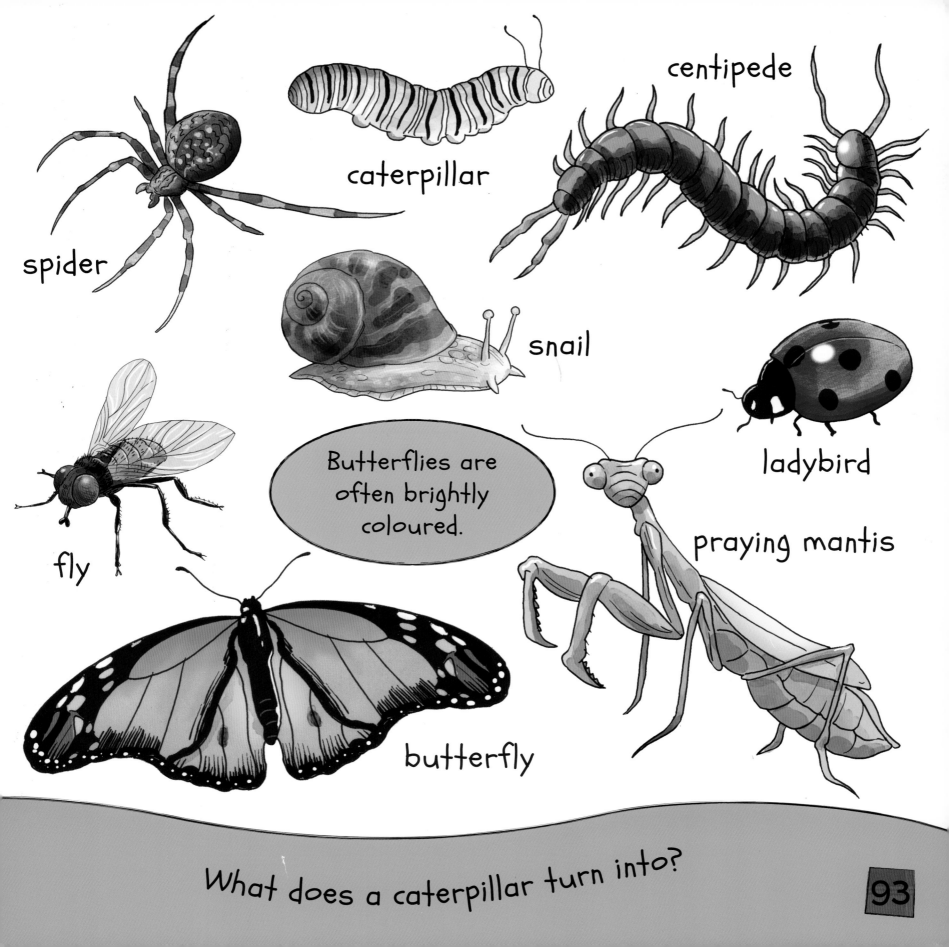

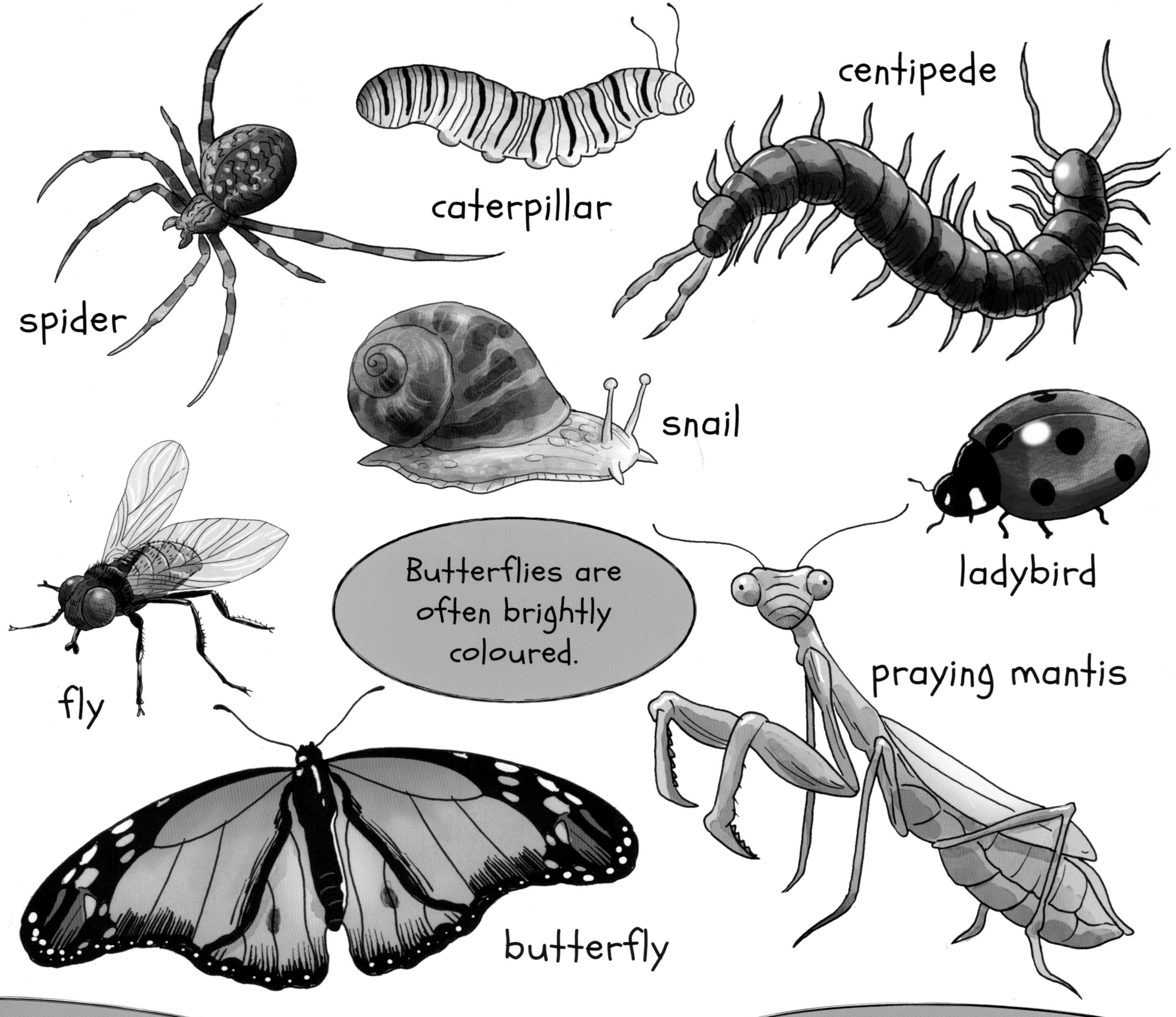

Pets

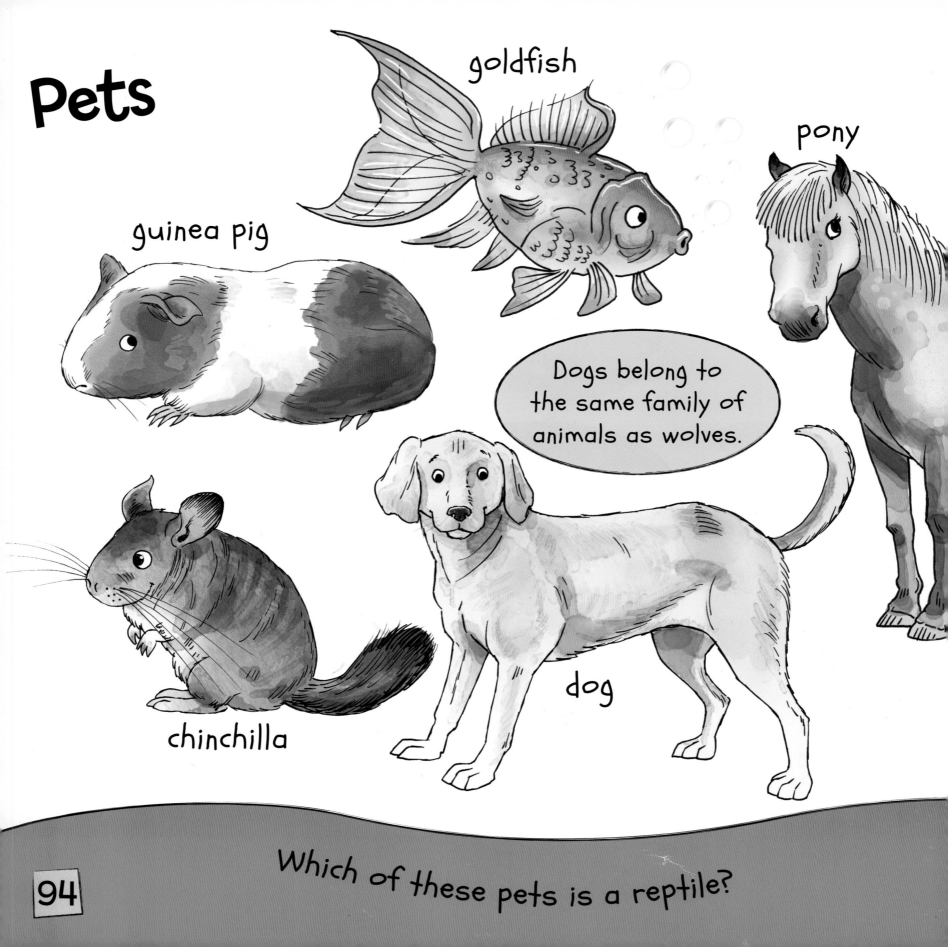

Dogs belong to the same family of animals as wolves.

Which of these pets is a reptile?

tortoise

rabbit

gerbil

budgerigar

cat

hamster

Budgerigars are also called budgies.

Which of these pets do you have?

Can you find?

Look back on pages 74–95 to see if you can find the following animals.

giant panda

tree frog

crab

octopus

hippopotamus

duck

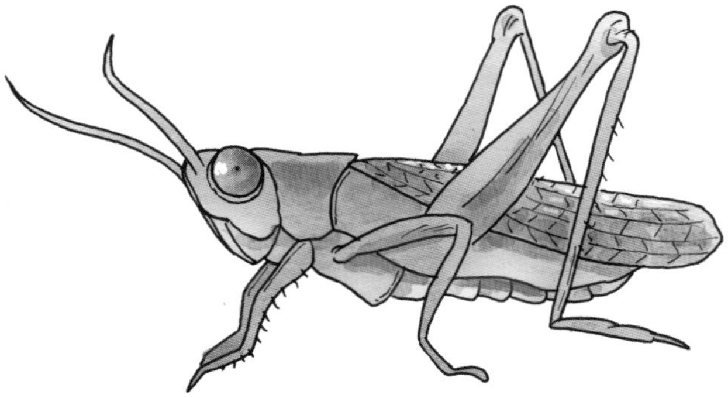

grasshopper

goldfish

12 1 2 3 4 6 7 8 9 10 11